Your
Amazing
Feelings!

Library of Congress Control Number:
2024907643

Published on Amazon by John Pritchett

Your Amazing Feelings!

Hey! Did you know your feelings are like mini superheroes hiding inside you? Yep, they wear tiny capes and everything! Learning to understand and take care of them is like getting your own set of superpowers. And guess what? You're about to be a feelings superhero!

Imagine all the feelings you have— like when you're jumping-for-joy happy, or when you're feeling like a grumpy cat, or maybe even when you're scared of that mysterious sound at night. Each feeling is like a special tool on your superhero utility belt.

And here's the funny part: sometimes these feelings have a mind of their own! Like when happiness decides to show up during math class or when grumpiness sneaks in because you have to eat veggies. But that's okay! Even superheroes have off days.

The best part? Feeling all sorts of emotions is totally okay and normal. It's like having a wardrobe full of superhero

costumes—one for every occasion! And

when you learn to talk about and handle

these feelings, you're basically getting

your superhero training.

Get ready to wear your emotional

cape with pride! This book is packed with

cool tips and tricks to help you

understand and manage all your feelings.

You'll learn fancy words to describe

them and ways to express yourself like

a true feelings superhero.

So, buckle up, little superhero! It's time to explore the wild and wacky world of feelings. Are you ready for this epic adventure? "On your mark, get set. Let's go!"

Your Warm Heart

Alright, little heroes, let's gear up in our superhero capes and uncover those heroic moments that warm our hearts!

The Smile Clue. Imagine you're a superhero spotting clues. Watch out for your smile! When happiness fills the air, your face might shine brighter than a superhero's beacon. It's like discovering a hidden treasure—the smile is your superpower evidence!

The Heartbeat Mystery.
Superheroes have super senses. Listen
to your heartbeat! When joy fills your
veins, your heart might drum a heroic
tune, like it's vanquished a villain. Tune
in—it's your heart's heroic signal saying,
"Mission accomplished!"

The Giggle Trail. Follow the
giggles, young hero! When happiness
strikes, you might burst into giggles.
It's like tracking footprints left by a

friendly giant. Follow the laughter, and you're on the path to heroism!

The Energy Detective. Heroes are powered by energy. When happiness energizes you, you'll feel as lively as a superhero in flight. If you're bouncing or dancing, your joy-o-meter is skyrocketing, superhero style!

Friendship Evidence. Heroes cherish their allies. Look around—are your superhero buddies nearby? If you're teaming up, sharing secrets, or having a blast, that's the hero's code of happiness. Friends are your trusty sidekicks in your superhero journey!

The Gratitude Clue. Heroes are grateful for their blessings. Reflect on what brings you joy—a cool gadget, a sunny day, or a favorite pet. Gratitude is your superhero magnifying glass—it reveals the power of happiness hidden within.

The Adventure Trail. Heroes are born adventurers. If you're exploring new frontiers, testing your limits, or feeling like an intrepid explorer, you're on a heroic quest of happiness! It's like navigating a magical map to wonderful place.

Being a happiness hero means keeping your senses sharp for these heroic clues. So, keep your hero journal at the ready, and when you spot these signs, give yourself a superhero high-five—you've cracked the happiness case wide open! Keep shining your heroic light, little champions!

Now, let's elevate our hero game and learn how to share happiness with the world!

The Joyful Report. Picture this— you're a superhero unveiling a mystery. When happiness fills your heart, share your superhero discovery! Tell your friends and family what made you beam. It's like announcing, "Superhero [Your

Name] on duty: I've unearthed a joy gem!"

The High-Five Clue. Heroes revel in triumphs. Slap someone a high-five! It's like declaring, "We've unlocked the fun achievement!" High-fives are the heroic handshake of happiness.

The Gratitude Note. Scribble a thank-you message. Heroes leave behind clues, right? So, put your pen to paper and scribble a thank you note, "Dear [Friend's Name], your kindness supercharged my joy!" It's like sprinkling magical hero dust.

The Happy Dance. Imagine this— you've cracked a riddle worthy of a superhero's brain. Now, groove like a hero! Wiggle, twirl, and strut your joy. It's like leaving a heroic trail of delight.

The Giggle Code. Whisper a rib-tickling joke or a goofy secret. Superheroes share secrets with their trusty allies. Lean in and say, "Hey, why did the chicken join the band? It had the perfect egg-shaker!" Giggles are the secret handshake of happiness.

The Hug Evidence. Heroes gather heartwarming evidence. Offer someone a snug embrace—it's like declaring, "I've got undeniable proof of happiness right here!" Hugs are the hero's heart-shaped clues.

The Smile Cipher. Flash that heroic smile! Superheroes are adept at decoding secret messages. Your grin broadcasts, "Mission accomplished—I'm radiating joy!" It's the universal language of superhero happiness.

So, remember, happiness heroes sprinkle joy like magical pixie dust wherever they soar. Don your superhero cape, harness your inner powers, and let's heroically unravel those happiness clues!

Your Brave Lighthouse

Alright, little heroes, let's imagine your heart as a brave lighthouse, standing tall on the shores of your feelings. Just like a lighthouse guides ships through stormy waters, your heart's lighthouse helps you to steer through your feelings.

The Blinking Light. Think of your lighthouse light spinning, shining brightly, and then fading. When you're feeling sad, it blinks faster, like a little superhero alerting you: "Something's not right!"

So, be a vigilant superhero and notice that blinking light inside you. If it's blinking a lot, it's like your heart's way of saying, "I might be feeling sad, heroes!"

The Stormy Sea of Feelings. Imagine your feelings as mighty waves crashing against your heroic lighthouse. When sadness strikes, those waves grow wilder. Your emotional sea feels stormy and choppy.

Listen closely to those emotional waves—they'll give you clues about your feelings.

The Lonely Lighthouse. Sometimes, when sadness clouds your heart, it feels like your heart's lighthouse is a lone hero standing on a cliff. It feels a bit lonely, just like our brave lighthouse by the sea.

So, if you ever feel like your heart's a lone hero on a cliff, it might mean you're feeling sad.

The Light in the Dark. Remember, heroes shine their light even in the darkest times. When sadness tries to dim your glow, your heart's lighthouse still beams, trying to show you the way.

Search for that brave light within you—it's your heart declaring, "I'm feeling sad, but I'm still shining!"

The Safe Harbor. Lighthouses keep sailors safe and sound. When sadness rocks your boat, your heart's lighthouse is like a welcoming harbor. It whispers, "Come here, little hero. Seek shelter with me."

So, if you ever need comfort, picture your heart's lighthouse offering you a safe haven to recharge.

Heroes, it's totally okay to feel sad sometimes. Your heart's lighthouse is always there to guide you through those stormy feelings. Talk to a trusted sidekick and let them know if your lighthouse is blinking a lot. Remember, you're not alone!

Using Your Lighthouse to Signal Others. Turn on Your Light. Just like a lighthouse shines its beacon to guide ships, let your inner light shine through. When you're feeling down, your face might look a bit gloomy, or your smile might fade. People around you will notice and want to help.

Send Out Signals. Lighthouses blink to send messages. You can do the same! Use your words to say, "I'm feeling a bit blue today." It's like sending out a superhero distress signal: "Hey, my lighthouse needs some backup!"

Share Your Stormy Sea. Imagine your feelings as waves crashing against your lighthouse. When you're sad, share your stormy sea with someone you trust.

Say, "I'm feeling sad because..." Sharing lightens the load.

Ask for a Lifeboat. Lighthouses don't sail alone; they have lifeboats nearby. When you're feeling low, ask for a lifeboat—a listening ear or a comforting hug. Say, "Can we talk? I need a little superhero support."

Paint Your Lighthouse Window. Sometimes, lighthouses change their light color to signal danger. You can do something similar! Wear a blue shirt or draw a sad face. People will notice and ask, "What's wrong, hero?"

Be a Beacon for Others. Heroes guide others too. If you see a fellow hero feeling sad, be their guiding light. Say, "I'm here for you. Let's navigate this together."

Keep Your Light On. Even when sadness tries to dim your glow, keep your inner light shining bright. It's okay to be sad sometimes. Your light helps others find their way, too.

So, keep being the brave heroes

you are, and let your heart's lighthouse

guide you through the highs and lows of

feelings!

Your Fiery Dragon

Alright, young heroes, let's imagine that our anger is like a fiery dragon inside us. When you're angry, it's like that dragon breathes hotter and brighter flames. Here's how you can recognize when you're angry.

Heat Within. Picture your body as having a tiny dragon's den. When you're angry, that dragon stokes up the heat! Your face might feel warm, and your heart beats faster—just like a dragon's fiery breath.

Red Flames. Imagine your anger as a dragon's flame. When you're angry, this flame turns fiery red. It's like your insides are burning with frustration or irritation. So, if you feel like you're seeing red, it's a sign your inner dragon is angry!

Smoke Signals. Just as smoke rises from a dragon's fiery breath, your body sends signals. Pay attention to tightness in your shoulders, clenched fists, or a racing heartbeat. These are like little smoke signals saying, "Hey, my dragon is feeling mad!"

Dragon Roar Thoughts. Close your eyes and listen. When you're angry, it's like there's a dragon roaring in your head. Thoughts race, and you might want to stomp your feet or yell—just like a dragon's roar echoing in the mountains.

Burning Words. Imagine your words as sparks flying out of a dragon's mouth. When you're angry, those sparks can sting! You might say things you don't mean or raise your voice. So, if your words feel like fiery sparks, it's a clue your inner dragon is upset. Saying you're sorry after an angry outburst is a superhero power.

Remember, feeling angry is normal, like having a fiery dragon inside. But just like we need to calm down a dragon's fiery temper, we need to learn how to calm our anger, too. Take deep breaths, count to ten, and let the flames cool down. You've got this brave dragon tamers!

Expressing Your Dragon Anger to Others.

The Dragon Roar Call. Picture a dragon roaring loudly when it's angry! Similarly, when you're mad, use your words like a dragon's roar. Say, "I'm feeling angry right now." It's like letting out a roar to signal to others that you need help.

The Dragon Alert. Imagine a little red dragon scale on your forehead. When you're angry, that scale glows like an emergency signal. People notice it and know you're upset and may need help. So, if you feel like your dragon alert is glowing, it's time to let others know.

The Dragon's Words of Warning. Think of your voice as a dragon's warning growl. When you're angry, let that growl out! Speak firmly but respectfully. Say, "I don't like that" or

"This makes me upset." It's like the dragon's growl warning others to back off.

The Dragon Whisper. Imagine whispering a secret to calm your dragon. When you're angry, say, "I need to talk." It's like whispering to a dragon whisperer—they'll listen and help you cool down. Remember, it's okay to ask for help when your inner dragon is roaring!

The Dragon's Cooling Breath. Just as a dragon can have a calming breath, your words can cool down anger. Take a deep breath and say, "Let's find a solution" or "Can we work this out?" It's like blowing a soothing breeze over your fiery dragon feelings.

The Dragon's Calming Potion Words. Imagine having a special potion of words. When you're angry, use those words to calm the dragon's flames. Say, "I'm upset because..." or "I need some space." It's like using a calming potion to soothe the fiery dragon inside!

Remember, expressing anger is like taming a fiery dragon. Use your words wisely, and soon the flames will settle. You've got this, little dragon tamers!

Your Alert System

Alright, young heroes, let's imagine your feelings are like a superhero alert system inside you. When you're afraid, that superhero alarm goes off, alerting you to pay attention!

Butterflies in Your Tummy. When you're scared, you might feel like there are little superhero butterflies fluttering around in your tummy. It's like the alarm saying, "Hey, something's not right! Danger alert!"

Heart Racing. Your heart might start beating faster. It's like the alarm ringing louder, saying, "Attention, attention! Be on the lookout for danger!"

Sweaty Palms. If your hands get sweaty, it's like the alarm saying, "Get ready to spring into action or find a safe spot!"

Wide Eyes. Your eyes might get big and wide, like the alarm flashing superhero-red lights, saying, "Stay alert, heroes!"

Shaky Legs. When you're afraid, your legs might feel a bit wobbly, just like the alarm making a loud noise, saying, "Heroes, assemble and be cautious!"

Remember, it's okay to feel afraid sometimes. Your superhero alarm helps you stay safe by telling you when to be cautious. And guess what? You can always ask a grown-up or another superhero for help if your alarm rings too loudly!

Letting Others Know When Your Superhero Alarm is Ringing.

Talk About It. Just like you'd tell someone if your superhero alarm was making a loud noise, talk to a grown-up or a superhero friend. Say, "I'm feeling scared right now." They'll listen and help you feel better.

Show Your Superhero Face. When you're afraid, your face might change. Your eyes might get big and wide, like the superhero alarm flashing bright red lights. Let your face show it!

Superheroes around you will notice and

ask what's wrong.

Ask for a Heroic Hug.

Sometimes, all you need is a comforting

hug. It's like turning off the superhero

alarm by getting a warm hug from

someone who cares about you.

Hold Hands. If you're scared,

hold someone's hand. It's like having a

superhero buddy to turn off the alarm

together. You'll feel safer and less afraid.

Use Your Heroic Words. Use your words to say, "I'm scared." It's like pressing the snooze button on your superhero alarm. When you say it out loud, superheroes around you will understand and help you feel better.

Remember, it's okay to feel afraid sometimes. Your superhero alarm helps you stay safe, and sharing your feelings with other superheroes makes it easier

to handle. Stay brave, little heroes!

Keeping Your Heart Smiling

Alright, young heroes, let's dive into the adventure of keeping your heart smiling all day long. Imagine your heart as a big, friendly superhero with a glowing smile inside you. Here's how to keep that superhero heart happy and smiling!

Kindness. Just like when you share your superhero gadgets or help a friend in need, your heart does a happy dance. Be kind to others—it's like giving your heart a heroic high-five!

Gratitude. When you say "thank you" or appreciate the little things, your heart feels like it's soaring through the skies. Remember to be thankful—it's like adding a shiny superhero shield to your heart.

Laughter. Laughing is like the best superpower for your heart! Watch funny superhero movies, tell jokes, or play with your pet sidekick. Your heart will laugh with joy, like a superhero saving the day!

Playtime. Run, jump, and play! When you're active, your heart feels like it's flying. So, go outside and let your heart play catch with the clouds!

Hugs. Hugs are magical—they make your heart feel invincible. Give hugs to your family, friends, and even your teddy bear. Your heart will beam like a sunshine superhero!

Dreams. Imagine your heart wearing a superhero cape. Dreams and hopes are like superpowers! Think about

49

what you want to achieve—it's like giving

your heart wings to fly.

Love. Love is the biggest heart-

smiler of all! Tell your family you love

them, and they'll send heart emojis

right back. Love makes your heart shine

brighter than any superhero signal!

Remember, your heart loves to

smile. So, sprinkle kindness, laughter,

and love all around—it's like giving your

superhero heart a bunch of colorful

balloons! Keep that heart-smile shining,

young heroes!

Your Gentle Cloud
of Sadness

Alright, young heroes, let's embark on a heroic journey to take care of ourselves when the gentle cloud of sadness drifts into our sky. Just like a cloud changes shape and moves, your sadness can shift too. Here's how to be your own superhero when that happens!

Talk to Someone. Imagine your cloud sharing its story with a fellow superhero. Talk to a friend, family member, or teacher. They're like superhero allies who listen to and understand your feelings.

Write It Down. Picture your cloud leaving a trail behind. Grab a superhero journal and write down your feelings. It's like giving your cloud a secret base to rest and recover.

Take Deep Breaths. Imagine inhaling superpower energy and exhaling the heaviness. Breathe slowly and deeply—it's like using your superhero strength to help your cloud float away.

Find Your Happy Place. Close your eyes and imagine a special place where your cloud feels lighter. Maybe it's a cozy superhero hideout, a sunny superhero beach, or a magical superhero forest. Spend time there in your mind and recharge your superpowers.

Draw or Paint. Picture your cloud turning into vibrant superhero colors. Grab some crayons or paints and create! Expressing your feelings through art is like turning your cloud into a heroic masterpiece.

Listen to Music. Imagine your cloud dancing to an uplifting superhero theme song. Put on your favorite music—it's like throwing a superhero dance party just for your cloud.

Hug a Stuffed Animal. Pretend your cloud is a soft, cuddly superhero sidekick. Hug your favorite stuffed animal—it's like sharing warmth, comfort, and superhero strength.

Go Outside. Imagine your cloud floating in the open superhero sky. Step outside, feel the breeze, and let the sun touch your face. Nature can lift your cloud and boost your superhero powers.

Remember, clouds come and go. Be your own superhero, be kind to yourself, and soon your cloud will drift away, leaving a clear superhero sky behind. Stay strong, young heroes!

Tackling Your Fiery Dragon

Hey there, young heroes! Ready to tackle that fiery dragon of anger inside you? Let's dive into some heroic tricks to tame that dragon!

Roar Softly. Instead of letting your dragon roar loudly, try roaring softly. Whisper or hum your favorite superhero theme song. It's like your dragon singing a calming lullaby to soothe its fiery spirit.

Find a Calm Spot. Imagine a secret superhero cave where your dragon can cool down and relax. Go there—maybe it's your room or a cozy superhero corner filled with your favorite comics and toys.

Count to Three Scales. Imagine your dragon has three shiny scales on its back. Count them silently: "One, two, three." By the time you finish counting, your dragon will feel less fiery and more at ease.

Taking a Break. If you notice your dragon getting angry, find a quiet superhero spot, take deep breaths, and calm down. Imagine you're blowing out your dragon's fiery anger with your superhero breath.

Breathe Fire Slowly. When your dragon feels angry, take deep breaths. Pretend you're breathing out fire, but do it slowly. Inhale deeply, hold it for a moment like a true superhero, and then exhale slowly. This helps cool down your dragon's flames.

Remember, even the mightiest dragons need to calm down sometimes. So, practice these heroic actions, and soon your inner dragon will be feeling better and ready to join you on your next epic adventure! Stay brave, young heroes!

Brave Knight

Hey there, young heroes! Picture yourself as a brave knight on an epic quest. Whenever fear tries to block your path, imagine it as a fiery dragon or a spooky monster lurking in the shadows. But don't worry—you've got a special shield, crafted from courage, deep breaths, and positive thoughts.

Raise Your Magical Shield. When fear breathes its fiery breath, raise your shield high! Take a deep breath, remind yourself of your bravery, and face that dragon or monster head-on! Remember, conquering fear is like learning to tame a friendly dragon that lives inside you.

Here are some heroic tricks to help you face your fears and conquer them:

Talk About It. Share your fears with someone you trust—a friend, family member, or teacher. Talking about it helps you feel less alone and more like a team of brave knights ready to face any challenge.

Make a List. Write down the things or situations that scare you. It's like shining a bright knight's light on those dark corners, making them less scary.

Break It Down. Imagine your fear as a big, challenging quest. Break it into smaller, manageable tasks. For example, if you're scared of the dark, start by leaving a nightlight on as your guiding

beacon.

Boost Realistic Thinking.
Challenge those spooky thoughts!

Instead of thinking, "There's a monster

under my bed," say to yourself,

"Monsters aren't real, and my bed is a

safe fortress."

Cheer Yourself On. Imagine

you're a brave knight charging into

battle. When you face fear, cheer

yourself on with a courageous shout: "I can do this! I am brave!"

Remember, every brave step you take shrinks that dragon or scary monster a little bit more, making it easier to conquer. Keep shining your brave knight's light and soon those fears will vanish like shadows in the sunlight! Stay courageous, young heroes!

Your Amazing Feelings!

Hey there, young superheroes!

Guess what? You've unlocked a superpower deep inside you that helps you understand, express, and manage all your incredible feelings. Just like a fearless explorer, you've discovered hidden emotional treasures within yourself and learned how to talk about your feelings in really awesome ways.

Imagine each emotion you feel— whether it's happiness, sadness, anger, or fear—as a unique color on your superhero palette. With this palette, you can paint a vibrant picture of your life's adventures. Understanding your feelings is like leveling up in the game of growing up strong and healthy.

Now that you've transformed into an Emotional Superhero, you've got some amazing strategies to tackle any feelings that come your way. So, keep showing that bravery, young adventurers! Keep learning, keep growing, and keep mastering the art of handling your feelings to accomplish truly heroic feats!

And here's a secret tip: the more you practice using your emotional superpowers, the stronger they'll become. Emotional intelligence is a super skill you'll use throughout your entire life, so it's awesome that you're getting a head start now. Keep soaring high, little heroes!

Other books by John Pritchett.

You Can Be a Hero Too!
You Can Be an Amazing Friend!
You Can Get Better at Anything!
You Can Do Amazing Yoga!
You Can Bee Healthy!

Made in the USA
Middletown, DE
04 September 2024

59738513R00042